CONTENTS

JANE AUSTEN – A BRIEF BIOGRAPHY

Jane Austen was born on 16 December 1775 at the rectory in the village of Steventon near Basingstoke in Hampshire. Jane was the seventh of eight children, and the second daughter, of the Reverend George Austen and his wife, Cassandra.

In 1783, at the age of seven, Jane and her sister Cassandra were sent off to be schooled with a small group of girls in Oxford and shortly afterwards in Southampton. Jane was young to be sent away to school; however the sisters were very close and their mother is reported to have said that 'if Cassandra's head had been going to be cut off, Jane would have hers cut off too'. The girls were brought home after an infectious disease broke out at the school. Jane caught the disease and nearly died. In 1785–6 Jane and Cassandra went away to school again, to the Ladies' Boarding School within the Abbey Gateway in Reading. These two short episodes were Jane's only education outside her home and family. Her father, her brothers and her father's extensive library supplied the remainder of her wide and, for the period, enlightened education.

Jane wrote for her family from an early age and enjoyed their pleasure in her work. The writings, collectively known as *The Juvenilia*, were written in three notebooks and included her first attempt at an epistolary novel, *Love and Freindship* (sic), which she wrote at the age of 14 and *A History of England by a partial, prejudiced and ignorant Historian,* which she wrote at 15.

In her late teens and early twenties Jane wrote the novels that were later to be reworked and published as *Sense and Sensibility*, *Pride and Prejudice* and *Northanger Abbey*.

Although Jane attended balls and other social occasions, she did not at this time receive any offers of marriage. A flirtation with Tom Lefroy was brought to an end as neither of the young people had the financial means to marry.

In 1801 Revd George Austen was approaching 70 and the work of the parish was putting a strain on him. It was decided that he would retire to Bath, vacating the Steventon living for his eldest son James. As unmarried daughters Cassandra and Jane had no choice but to

Left:
Steventon Rectory
Below: Bath

accompany their parents to Bath, where their lives would be very different from their Hampshire home. Jane loved the country, enjoyed long country walks and had many Hampshire friends. The announcement of the move must have come as a very unwelcome shock, especially when many of the family's possessions had to be sold off to help financially. The sale included the books of her father's library, the piano and much of Jane's sheet music.

The four years in Bath were largely unproductive ones for Jane.

In December 1802, while visiting friends in Hampshire, Jane did receive an offer of marriage when Harris Bigg-Wither proposed. At first Jane accepted this proposal; however after a sleepless night she withdrew her acceptance. Although the match would

have been advantageous to Jane and her family and would have secured their financial situation, had this marriage taken place Jane may not have written her novels.

More unhappiness and reduced circumstances were to follow when Revd Austen died unexpectedly on 21 January 1805.

After his death the income of the Austen women was in a delicate state. Mrs Austen and her daughters were forced to rely on the Austen sons for help. Shortly after Mr Austen's death, the Austen ladies and their friend Martha Lloyd moved to Southampton to share the home of Jane's naval brother Frank and his wife Mary.

Jane had written little in Bath and wrote nothing at all in Southampton.

In 1808 her brother Edward, who had been adopted by distant cousins Thomas and Catherine Knight, and had inherited estates in Hampshire and Kent, offered his mother and sisters a permanent home on his Chawton estate and the Austen ladies moved back to the Hampshire countryside in July 1809. Chawton represented a return to the landscape and a way of life that Jane had enjoyed in her years in Steventon; the place which had nurtured her early talent.

Above: Chawton Cottage
Below: Chawton House and St Nicholas Church

The cottage on Edward's estate was a comfortable house, with a pretty garden, and most importantly it provided the settled home that Jane needed in order to write.

It is not known to what extent Jane rewrote her early works once at Chawton, but it was certainly in her Chawton home that Jane prepared all of her manuscripts for publication. *Sense and Sensibility* was the first to be published in October 1811, followed by *Pride and Prejudice* in January 1813. Having been written entirely at Chawton *Mansfield Park* was published in 1814, followed by *Emma* in 1816. Jane then completed *Persuasion*, which was published together with *Northanger Abbey* in 1818, the year after her death. None of the books published in Jane's lifetime identified her as the author. *Sense and Sensibility* was described as being written 'By a Lady' and subsequent novels referred to Jane as the author of one of her previous books. Early in 1817 Jane started another novel *Sanditon*, but illness prevented her from completing it and the work was abandoned.

Jane had begun to feel unwell in 1816 but continued to work. No longer able to walk far, she used to drive out in their donkey carriage. She wrote in December to her nephew James Edward Austen

> ***'the walk is beyond my strength (though I am otherwise very well) & this is not the season for Donkey Carriages.'***

Although her final illness only overtook Jane in the last year of her life she may have been ill for some time. It is not possible to say with certainty what caused her death, however the latest suggested medical opinion is Bovine T.B. of the kidney, acquired from drinking unpasteurised milk. The symptoms are similar to those of Addison's disease which has previously been suggested. Another possibility is a lymphoma.

By May 1817 Jane was so ill that she and Cassandra rented rooms in a house in College Street in Winchester to be near Jane's physician, Mr Lyford. Jane left Chawton for the last time on 24 May.

> ***'My journey hither on Saturday was performed with very little fatigue, & had it been a fine day I think I should have felt none, but it distressed me to see uncle Henry & Wm. K who kindly attended us on horseback, riding in rain almost all the way.'***

Whatever the illness there was no cure at the time and Jane died in Cassandra's arms in the early hours of 18 July 1817. She was 41 years old. Jane was buried in Winchester Cathedral. Cassandra wrote to her niece Fanny,

> ***'I have lost a treasure, such a Sister, such a friend as never can be surpassed... The last sad ceremony is to take place on Thursday morning, her dear remains are to be deposited in the cathedral – it is satisfaction to me to think that they are to lie in a Building she admird so much.'***

Above: 8 College Street, Winchester
Below: Memorial marking Jane Austen's grave in Winchester Cathedral

In Memory of
JANE AUSTEN,
youngeſt daughter of the late
Revd GEORGE AUSTEN,
formerly Rector of Steventon in this County
ſhe departed this Life on the 18th of July 1817,
aged 41, after a long illneſs ſupported with
the patience and the hopes of a Chriſtian.

The benevolence of her heart,
the ſweetneſs of her temper, and
the extraordinary endowments of her mind
obtained the regard of all who knew her, and
the warmeſt love of her intimate connections.

Their grief is in proportion to their affection
they know their loſs to be irreparable,
but in their deepeſt affliction they are conſoled
by a firm though humble hope that her charity,
devotion, faith and purity have rendered
her ſoul acceptable in the ſight of her
REDEEMER.

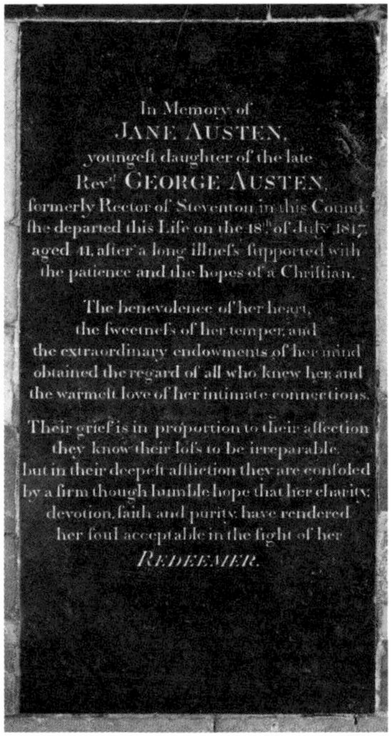

A TIMELINE OF THE LIFE OF JANE AUSTEN

JANE'S LIFE AND WORKS

- **1775, 16 December** Born at Steventon Rectory, near Basingstoke, Hampshire.
- **1783** At school in Oxford with her sister Cassandra under Mrs Crawley.
- **1783** School moved to Southampton. While here Jane nearly died of a 'putrid sore throat'.
- **1785–6** Jane and Cassandra attend school in Reading.
- **1790** *Love and Freindship* [sic] written.
- **1791** *The History of England by a partial, prejudiced and ignorant historian* written with illustrations by Cassandra.
- **1792** *Lesley Castle* written, followed by other youthful compositions.

THE AUSTEN FAMILY

- **1779** Charles John Austen (Jane's brother) born at Steventon.
- **1783** Edward Austen adopted by Mr and Mrs Thomas Knight of Godmersham, Kent.
- **1786** Francis Austen leaves the Royal Naval Academy and sails to the East Indies.
- **1789** Publication of the first issue of James Austen's periodical *The Loiterer*; issued weekly until March 1790.
- **1790** James Austen takes up residence as curate of Overton, Hampshire.
- **1791** Charles Austen enters the Royal Naval Academy.
- **1791** James Austen becomes vicar of Sherborne St John, Hampshire.
- **1791** Edward Austen marries Elizabeth Bridges.
- **1792** James Austen marries Anne Mathew; they move to the parsonage in Deane.
- **1792** Cassandra Austen engaged to Revd Tom Fowle.
- **1793** Henry Austen becomes a lieutenant in the Oxfordshire Militia.

1775 | 1780 | 1785 | 1790

LITERARY AND POLITICAL HISTORY

- **1775** American War of Independence begins with the Battle of Lexington.
- **1776** American Declaration of Independence.
- **1778** Publication of Frances Burney's novel *Evelina.*
- **1783, December.** William Pitt the Younger becomes Prime Minister of Great Britain.
- **1788** First edition of *The Times* is published.
- **1788** Beginning of the Regency Crisis, caused by King George III's madness.
- **1789** Publication of William Blake's poems *Songs of Innocence.*
- **1789** Storming of the Bastille in Paris signals beginning of French Revolution.
- **1791** Publication of James Boswell's biography *Life of Johnson.*
- **1793** Execution of Louis XV and Marie Antoinette.

JANE'S LIFE AND WORKS

- **1795–6** Jane first meets Tom Lefroy.
- **1797**, **October**. *First Impressions* completed (subsequently *Pride and Prejudice* when published).
- **1797** *First Impressions* rejected by Cadell publishers.
- **1797–8** *Susan* written (later named *Northanger Abbey* when published).
- **1802** Proposal of marriage from Harris Bigg-Wither, accepted that evening, but after a sleepless night turned down the following morning.
- **1803** *Susan* sold by Jane's father to Benjamin Crosby and advertised, but not then printed.
- **1804** *The Watsons* started. This novel was never completed.
- **1805** *Lady Susan* (different story to *Susan*) completed.
- **1805**, **21 January**. Death of her father Revd George Austen and his burial at Bath.
- **1809**, **7 July**. Arrival at Chawton and move into the house provided by her brother Edward from his inheritance of the estate of Thomas Knight.
- **1809** Unsuccessful attempt to revive publication of *Susan*.

THE AUSTEN FAMILY

- **1794** Eliza de Feuillide's husband is guillotined in Paris.
- **1797** James Austen marries Mary Lloyd.
- **1797** Tom Fowle dies of fever in San Domingo and is buried at sea.
- **1797** Henry Austen marries Eliza de Feuillide.
- **1799** Austen's aunt, Mrs Leigh-Perrot, charged with shoplifting.
- **1801** Austen family moved from Steventon to Bath on her father's retirement as Rector.
- **1801** James Austen becomes curate at Steventon.
- **1806** Moved with mother and sister from Bath to join her brother Francis in Southampton.

1795 | **1800** | **1805** | **1810**

LITERARY AND POLITICAL HISTORY

- **1794** Robespierre is executed and the Reign of Terror ends.
- **1794** Publication of William Blake's poems *Songs of Experience.*
- **1797** Publication of Ann Radcliffe's novel *The Italian.*
- **1798** Publication of William Wordsworth and Samuel Taylor Coleridge's poems *Lyrical Ballads.*
- **1804** Napoleon crowns himself emperor of the French.
- **1804** Publication of William Blake's poem *Jerusalem.*
- **1805** Battle of Trafalgar
- **1807** Publication of William Wilberforce's *A Letter on the Abolition of the Slave Trade.*

JANE'S LIFE AND WORKS

- **1811** *Sense and Sensibility* 'by a Lady' accepted and published by Thomas Egerton through negotiations by her brother Henry.
- **1813** *Pride and Prejudice* 'by the author of Sense and Sensibility' published by Egerton.
- **1814** *Mansfield Park* written, and published by Egerton.
- **1815** *Emma* completed. Jane starts *Persuasion*.
- **1815** Austen visits the Prince Regent's Library at Carlton House; receives invitation to dedicate a future work to him.
- **1815** *Emma* published by John Murray and dedicated to HRH the Prince Regent.
- **1815–16** *Persuasion* written by 18 July 1816.
- **1817** Uncompleted draft of *Sanditon* – first twelve chapters only written.
- **1817, 24 May**. Jane moved to lodging rooms on first floor of a house in College Street, Winchester for treatment by physician Mr Lyford.
- **1817, 15 July.** Composition of poem *Venta* about Winchester races and St Swithun, patron saint of Winchester.
- **1817, 18 July**. Jane died in Winchester aged 41 years, with her sister Cassandra present.
- **1817, 24 July**. Her burial in the North Aisle of Winchester Cathedral.
- **1818** *Northanger Abbey* and *Persuasion* published posthumously by her brother Revd Henry Austen.

THE AUSTEN FAMILY

- **1812** Edward Austen officially adopts "Knight" as surname.
- **1816** Manuscript and copyright of unpublished *Northanger Abbey* recovered from Crosby for £10 by her brother Henry – without disclosing the real authorship.
- **1816** Henry's bank fails and he leaves London.
- **1820** Henry Austen marries Eleanor Jackson.

1815 **1820**

LITERARY AND POLITICAL HISTORY

- **1810** George III recognized as insane.
- **1811** George, Prince of Wales becomes Prince Regent.
- **1811** Luddites protest against industrialisation in Britain.
- **1812** Publication of the first Cantos of Lord Byron's poem *Childe Harold's Pilgrimage.*
- **1812** *The Swiss Family Robinson* by Johann David Wyss published.
- **1814** Napoleon abdicates and is exiled to Elba.
- **1815** Battle of Waterloo.
- **1817** *Rob Roy* by Sir Walter Scott published.
- **1818** *Frankenstein* by Mary Shelley published.

Hugh Thompson's illustration from Persuasion

Jane Austen's Family

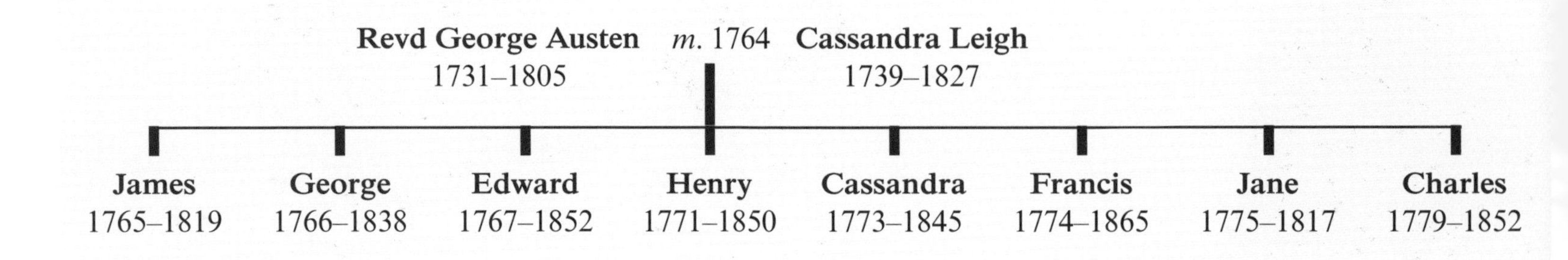

George Austen (1731–1805)

George Austen was born in 1731. He was orphaned in infancy when his mother died in childbirth with his youngest sister. His father died a year later. After living with various family members George earned a Fellowship to study at St John's, Oxford. He received a Bachelor of Arts, a Master of Arts and a Bachelor of Divinity degree. Known as 'the handsome proctor' he first met Cassandra Leigh in Oxford when she was visiting her uncle Theophilus. After they married, George became rector in several country parishes and they settled first in Deane and later at Steventon Rectory.

Cassandra Leigh Austen (1739–1827)

Cassandra Leigh Austen had family connections to Lord Leigh of Stoneleigh Abbey. It was while visiting her uncle, who was Master of Balliol College in Oxford, that Cassandra first met George Austen. Clever and witty, Cassandra Leigh Austen was from a higher social rank than her husband; however she was a good wife and mother and was held in great affection by her children.

James Austen

James Austen (1765–1819)

James, the eldest Austen son, went away to Oxford University in 1779 at the age of 14. He was ordained a clergyman in 1787. James wrote poetry and in 1789–90 edited (with Henry) a university magazine at Oxford called *The Loiterer*, which ran for sixty issues. James took over the living at Steventon vacated by his father's retirement. 3 children.

George Austen (1766–1838)

Not much is known of the Austen's second son, George, who suffered some form of mental handicap the details of which are not known. George lived most of his life with another family in Monks Sherborne, a village about twelve miles from Steventon. No children.

Edward Austen Knight (1767–1852)

Edward was adopted as their heir by Thomas and Catherine Knight. He was sent by his adoptive parents on the 'grand tour' of Europe in 1786–88, and eventually inherited their estates of Godmersham in Kent and Chawton in Hampshire. Edward took on the surname Knight in 1812. 11 children.

Henry Thomas Austen (1771–1850)

Henry was reputed to be Jane's favourite brother. Like his brother James he entered Oxford in 1788. Henry had several careers including serving in the Oxfordshire Militia. rising from lieutenant to captain, founding the bank Austen, Maunde & Tilson, which failed in 1816, and becoming a clergyman. Henry oversaw the publication of Jane's novels and wrote the first 'Biographical Notice' of his sister included in the posthumously published *Northanger Abbey* and *Persuasion*

He married his widowed cousin Eliza de Feuillide in 1797 and Eleanor Jackson in 1820. No children.

Cassandra Elizabeth Austen (1773–1845)

In a particularly affectionate family there seems to have been a special link between Cassandra and her sister Jane. Cassandra did become engaged to Thomas Fowle, a former pupil of her father; however he died on an expedition to the Caribbean and she never married.

Cassandra destroyed many of Jane's letters in her old age. She lived alone in Chawton after the death of her mother in 1827 until her own death in 1845, aged 72. She is buried at St Nicholas Church, Chawton alongside her mother. No children.

Above: Edward Knight
Left: Francis Austen
Below: Charles Austen

Francis William Austen (1774–1865)

Francis Austen served in the Royal Navy from the age of 12, rose to the position of Admiral of the Fleet and was knighted. Considered by Admiral Nelson to be 'an excellent young man', he narrowly missed involvement in the battle of Trafalgar due to being sent to Gibraltar for supplies for the fleet on Nelson's orders. After the death of his first wife Mary, Francis married Jane's friend Martha Lloyd in 1828. 11 children.

Charles John Austen (1779–1852)

Charles Austen entered the Royal Naval Academy in 1791 at the age of 12 and rose at the end of his career to the rank of Rear Admiral. Charles was stationed for seven years in the West Indies where he met and married his first wife Frances Palmer. Charles died of cholera, at age 73, still on active duty, during a naval river-war in Burma.

Jane referred to Charles as 'our own particular little brother' and it was from Charles that Jane and Cassandra received gifts of topaz crosses. 8 children.

Chawton Village

Above: Prowtings before it was altered and re-fronted

The village of Chawton has changed little over the centuries. The village was described in the Domesday Book and was in existence before this time. Today the village has approximately the same number of residents as in Jane's time; however there are more houses and fewer people per household.

If you go for a walk around the village it is possible to spot a number of buildings that Jane and her family would have known and visited.

BAIGENS

One of the oldest houses in the village and is believed to have been built in the early sixteenth century. The name of the house derives from the name of the family who lived in the house for many years. The house was sold to Edward Knight in 1869 at which time the original timber frame was built around with an outer brickwork shell.

ALPHONSUS HOUSE

Captain Benjamin Clement RN lived here from 1811 after his marriage to Ann Mary Prowting. He was the son of an Alton solicitor and related by marriage to Edward Gray, a partner in Henry Austen's Alton bank.

PROWTINGS

The Prowting family, who lived here in the early nineteenth century, were friends of the Austen family and are mentioned several times in Jane's letters. For upwards of two hundred years the Prowtings were first copyholders and then freeholders in the parish.

CLINKERS

Clinkers was originally two cottages and is believed to date from the mid sixteenth century with additions made to the house in Jane's time. The Clinker family had a blacksmith's shop here and in 1814 Jane wrote that 'the coach was stopped at the blacksmith's'.

CHAWTON HOUSE

Chawton House is a grade ll listed Elizabethan manor house. It was formerly owned by Jane Austen's brother, Edward Austen Knight, and later became the home of his eldest son. It is now The Centre for the Study of Early English Women's Writing, 1600–1830.

Dating back to before the Norman invasion the Manor of Chawton came into the hands of the Knight family in 1551 when the land was sold for £180 to John Knight, whose family had been tenant farmers in Chawton since the thirteenth century. The medieval manor house was replaced by John Knight's grandson, also called John, with the largely Elizabethan house that can be seen today.

In 1781, Thomas Knight II inherited Chawton House but as he and his wife Catherine had no children they made Edward Austen, son of Thomas's cousin Revd George Austen, their heir. Edward Austen Knight took over management of the Chawton estate in 1797, though he lived mostly in Kent at his other estate, Godmersham. The Great House at Chawton, as it was known, was let to gentlemen tenants including, for a number of years, one of Jane's other brothers, Francis.

Above: Chawton House from the south lawn
Below: St Nicholas Church, rebuilt in 1871

ST NICHOLAS CHURCH

A church has stood on the site of the present St Nicholas since at least 1270; however, a place of worship existed there before that date. The building was enlarged and improved inside in the early Victorian period; however, a disastrous fire in 1871 destroyed the majority of the building. Although Jane would regularly have worshipped at St Nicholas, only part of this building is as she would have known it.

Jane's mother and sister are buried in the churchyard and there are marble plaques to them inside the building.

The House

The cottage in Chawton was not always a part of the wider Chawton estates. The history of the ownership can be traced back to John Alderslade, owner of a successful ale brewing business in Alton, who purchased the cottage and garden freehold in 1624. It is believed, however, that the core of the house was built in the mid 1500s.

During the ownership of the Alderslade family significant improvements were made to create the house we see today. The previous house was not demolished but rather built around, doubling the thickness of the walls and extending the footprint of the house. It was extended to provide an additional room downstairs (the Drawing Room) as well as having the thatch roof removed and a full height first floor, with loft above, built over the new extended frontage.

By 1690 the Alderslades' investment in their home provided a smart house frontage with ground floor windows well spaced either side of a central front door opening directly onto the Winchester Road. The first floor had five front-facing windows. The whole structure had a sloping tiled front roof. At the rear of the house the roof was formed of four gables with valleys.

The house was acquired by Thomas Knight in 1769. As well as their manor house, Chawton House, and surrounding lands, the Knight family already owned most of the village. The house became an Inn at this time and later the home of the Chawton estate bailiff Bridger Seward.

Mr Seward continued with improvements to the house during his tenure. The separate kitchen was extended to adjoin the main house, though no internal doorway was provided to connect the two parts of the building. The kitchen itself was by now the main cooking part with a range; a partition door led to the 'back kitchen' (now the staff room) used for washing and preparation. This side wing of the house was built up to a two-storey height with a tiled roof. This did not extend the whole length of the wing but sloped down over the back kitchen.

The house was inherited along with the rest of the Chawton estate by Thomas Knight's son, also Thomas, in 1781 and later passed to Jane's brother Edward as part of his inheritance following his adoption into the Knight family.

It was because of the death of Bridger Seward in February 1808 that Edward (Austen) Knight was able to offer the cottage in Chawton to his mother and sisters. Edward offered them a choice of accommodation on his estates either in Kent or Hampshire. Mrs Austen initially may have been inclined to take the house in Wye on the Godmersham estate; however the family already knew the village of Chawton and appreciated its proximity to Alton where Henry Austen had a branch of his bank. Chawton was also less than fifteen miles from their much loved old home of Steventon where James now held the living.

Jane wrote to Cassandra about the house from Southampton:

> *'We are all quite familiarised to the idea ourselves; my mother only wants Mrs Seward to go out at Midsummer... Mrs J.A. expresses her fear of our settling in Kent and till this proposal was made, we began to look forward to it here... it will be best, however, as it is.'*
>
> **Letter to Cassandra, Monday 24 October 1808**

> *'There are six Bedchambers at Chawton; Henry wrote to my Mother the other day, and luckily mentioned the number – which is just what we wanted to be assured of. He also speaks of Garrets for store places...'*
>
> **Letter to Cassandra, Monday 20 November 1808**

Jane, Cassandra, their mother and their friend, Martha Lloyd, moved to Chawton on 7 July 1809.

Shortly after their arrival Jane wrote to her brother Francis a verse which included the lines:

> *'Our Chawton home how much we find*
> *Already in it to our mind;*
> *And how convinced that when complete*
> *It will all other houses beat*
> *That ever have been made or mended*
> *With rooms concise or*
> *Rooms distended.'*

Edward made further changes to the house to ensure the comfort of his mother and sisters including blocking up the window facing the road in the Drawing Room. The deep multi-pane shuttered sash window overlooking the garden was created to replace it.

Brickwork showing the previous line of the building, which was extended after 1845

Book shelves were fitted on the inside of the closed-up window. There is evidence that wallpaper was used to decorate the Drawing Room, the Dining Parlour and Mrs Austen's bedroom walls. It may also have been at this time that the windows were replaced with the small leaded-light style ones, which are evident in parts of the house today. There was a general redecoration and the third line of Jane's poem implies that the builders may still have been around on the day they moved in!

The house, referred to by the family as 'the Cottage', was previously known as either 'Petty John' or the 'New Inn' though it does not seem to have had a formal name and is still referred to as 'late Inn' on land tax documents after Mrs Austen's death.

Jane spent only eight years of her life in Chawton but they were the most productive of her career. Mrs Austen and Cassandra continued to live in the Chawton cottage until their respective deaths in 1827 and 1845. It is possible to visit their graves in the churchyard of St Nicholas Church.

After Cassandra's death the house was neglected at first and later divided into three cottages for workers of the Chawton estate.

The census returns for Chawton do not identify individual houses until 1881 when the occupants of the three properties are shown as Rose French a widowed agricultural servant, John Wyeth, the Chawton estate carpenter living with his wife and family of eight children, and James Gillet a farm labourer, also widowed.

Part of the building was used from as early as 1874 as a Working Men's Club, which included a Reading Room. The club later became known as The Workman's Improvement Club and later still as the St Nicholas Club.

After the building had been purchased in 1948 and was beginning to be turned into a museum there were still three tenants in the houses; Mrs Ethel Newman, the King family and Miss Annie Stevens and her widowed sister Mrs Ethel Wootton. In 1953 alternative accommodation was provided for Mrs Wootton and Miss Stevens forewent the 'use of these rooms'. In 1954 another house was purchased for Mr and Mrs King, and Mrs Newman moved to live with her daughter, therefore making the whole building available for use as the museum for the first time.

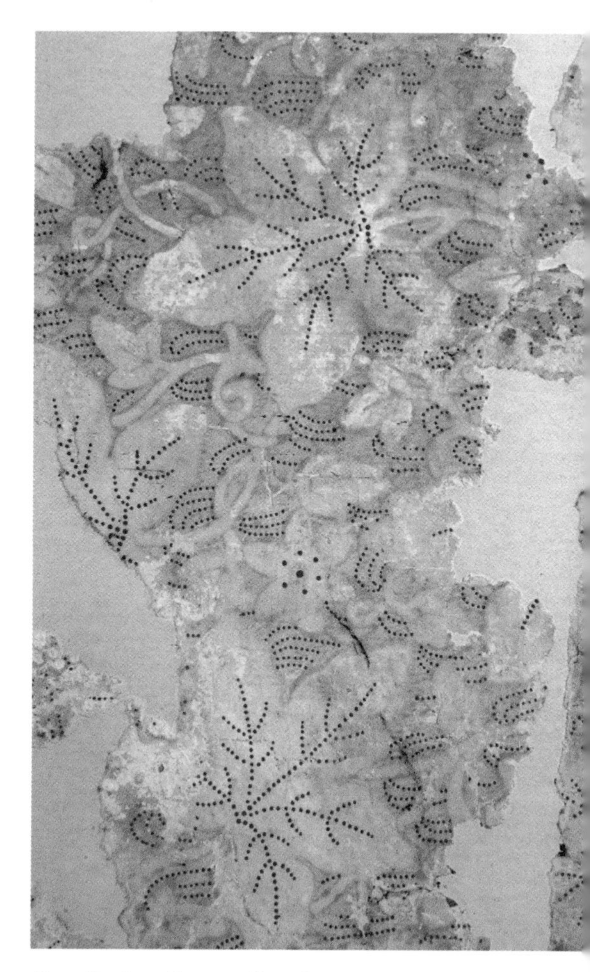

Detail of wallpaper, found during museum renovations

Opening of the Museum, July 1949

FROM COTTAGE TO MUSEUM

In 1947 Edward Knight, great-grandson of Jane's brother Edward Austen Knight, needed to sell by auction much of his Chawton Manor estate, including the cottage that had once been Jane's home. Miss Dorothy Darnell and her sister Miss Beatrix Darnell, who had established the Jane Austen Society in 1940 with the aim of being able to purchase the cottage to provide a memorial to Jane Austen and her work, wrote to *The Times* newspaper inviting donations to a fund they were raising in hope of acquiring the house. This letter was seen by Mr T Edward Carpenter JP, a retired solicitor in Mill Hill in London.

As there was insufficient time before the auction to raise an adequate bidding fund, Mr Carpenter negotiated purchasing the house and garden out of the Manor estate privately. The freehold purchase of the property took place in May 1948 for the sum of £3,000. The appeal for funds by the Jane Austen Society raised a further £1,400, which was spent on restoration work of the cottage.

Mr Carpenter presented the house to the nation in memory of his son Lieutenant Philip John Carpenter, who fell in battle in Lake Trasimene in June 1944.

(1)

61, High Street,
Alton, Hants,

46/C/1

16th January, 1947

Dear Sir,

Jane Austen Society.

The Committee of the Jane Austen Society have handed us your letter of the 8th January and asked us to ascertain from you exactly what your proposal is. We think we ought, before doing so, to answer your question with regard to full particulars of the property, and its letting.

The house is divided into four portions. Three are let to tenants at 2/6d a week and the other part to the village library who pay a nominal rent of 15/- a year. The three tenants cannot of course be made to vacate under present circumstances, although they are paying a very small rent.

Possession of the portion let to the village library can be obtained probably in less than six months, and it is this portion that the Society wish to get hold of, as soon as possible.

According to a report which the Society have received from their architects, there is a considerable amount of repair which ought to be taken in hand as soon as possible.

...stand you propose purchasing the property for £3000 and settling ...der to the Jane Austen Trustees. We ... take the income

In order to set up and run the house as a museum, Mr Carpenter formed the separate Jane Austen Memorial Trust as a registered education charity. This Trust has run and administered the house and its collection to the present day.

With a permanent home available for the first time, the museum's collection began to grow, including objects purchased, donated or loaned.

The Museum was formally opened on 23 July 1949.

The Times reported

> ***'The Duke of Wellington, opening the Museum – the occasion also commemorated the 132nd anniversary of Jane Austen's death – said that Lady Catherine de Bourgh would have discharged his task so well as to put him "in the blush" although she might have thought her time was wasted on a literary character.'***

On opening the Museum had few of Jane's personal possessions. Those housed originally as reported by *The Times* newspaper were 'two silk purses, a kerchief which she embroidered, her oak desk, and a piece of doggerel she wrote on having a pain in the head'.

The first door stewards of the Museum were the widowed ladies living in the house, but when they retired elsewhere the whole of the buildings and site then became available for museum use, with one wing provided for a steward, and eventually a Curator's on-site residence. Mr Carpenter travelled down from London each week, and undertook many tasks himself, including gardening.

After Mr Carpenter died in 1969 Elizabeth Rose, sister of Edward Knight, became the live-in steward for the next ten years. Mrs Rose made the house and visitors feel they really were just visiting someone's home.

On her retirement in 1979 her younger sister Ann Coates and her husband John became the first Curators. Over the next decade a full architect-supervised conservation overhaul of the structures on the site was undertaken, initially under the direction of John Coates.

The Centenary Plaque

In 1917, thirty years before the cottage was purchased to become a museum, the Alton Gazette highlighted the fact that there was no permanent memorial to Jane in Chawton to mark the years she had lived in the village and from which 'all her works were sent out into the world'. It was felt that the 100th anniversary of her death would be an appropriate occasion for marking 'in some distinctive way' her Chawton home.

The frame represents the pediment and pilasters of a window in 4 Sydney Place, Bath where Jane and her family lived from 1801 to 1804. The raised pattern on the oak surrounding the bronze plaque is copied from embroidery on a scarf worked by Jane. The idea was initiated by Miss Constance Hill and her words are those which are on the plaque.

Design: Miss E G Hill
Created by: Mr Evelyn Simmons, Lic RIBA. Organising Committee: Earl of Iddesleigh, Lord Latimer, Sir Frederick Pollock, Bart., Sir Robert Hudson, Sir William Robertson Nicoll, the Dean of Norwich, Mr Clarence Graff, Mr WD Howells, Mr WJ Locke and Mr CK Shorter.

'The aim of the Jane Austen Society is to acquire Chawton Cottage and while keeping it in repair and the main part of it in use as living accommodation, to make those rooms which are definitely associated with Jane Austen accessible to the public. Although there can be no question at present of vacant possession of the whole house, the Society will be able to get possession of the drawing-room which would make an ideal nucleus for the place of pilgrimage the Society hopes to establish. The Committee of the Society are trying to raise £5,000 for this purpose and are making this appeal for contributions towards the amount of admirers of Jane Austen's works.'

Report from the *Hampshire Countryside* 1947

In 1984 Jean Bowden, a retired botanist from Kew Gardens and knowledgeable Austen enthusiast, became Curator. Jean Bowden reinterpreted and rearranged the collection which by this time had grown significantly from the original few objects held at the time of the Museum opening. During her time the bookshop was created in the house (now the Reading Room), and the previously unused outbuilding was adapted to become a meeting and exhibition space. This education room became known as The Granary. Jean Bowden also pushed forward a number of other improvements to the museum over the next few years working closely with architect Penelope Adamson.

On Jean's retirement in 1994, Tom Carpenter, grandson of the Trust's founder, became the on-site Trustee responsible for administration and curatorial functions. His sister, Mrs Catherine Dean, is also a Trustee of the Memorial Trust.

In May 2003 Louise West joined the Museum as the first Education Officer, and introduced the schools' visit programme. She quickly became involved in many other aspects of the Museum and is now the incumbent Curator and has the responsibility for the museum collection.

In 2006 a Heritage Lottery Fund 'Your Heritage' grant was obtained for a project to reinterpret the museum display in a logical way. In 2008 another grant from the Heritage Lottery Fund enabled a significant redevelopment of the museum. This development aimed to improve the visitor experience and involved removing all retail elements from the house so that it took on more the feeling of the home Jane shared with her mother and sister. The project also involved adapting The Granary to become the museum entrance and shop and the construction of a new Learning Centre discreetly sited behind the Bakehouse, and in a style wholly sympathetic with the other buildings. This development was completed in time for the Museum to celebrate the bicentenary anniversary of the Austen women's arrival to live in Chawton.

Books
"We began a China Tea... and I find it very good"

Jane Austen spent the last eight years of her life in this unpretentious cottage from 1809 until 1817.

It was in this house that Jane's genius flourished and where she was free to write. She revised the three manuscripts she had written previously, but which remained unpublished, wrote three more novels and started one more, which was destined to remain unfinished before illness overtook her.

The Museum today reflects the comfortable family home that the Austen women created while telling the story of their lives and Jane's work.

The Drawing Room

This room is the largest in the house and is where the Austen ladies would have spent time entertaining visitors as well as enjoying such pastimes as painting and sewing.

One of the improvements made to the house when the Austens moved to Chawton was the filling-in of the large window, which faced the road. (Evidence of the window can still be seen on the exterior of the house.) An elegant Regency window overlooking the garden was installed instead, ensuring the room was a bright, sunny place in the daytime and that the family were unobserved by passing coaches.

Jane wrote to Cassandra about the day she first received copies of *Pride and Prejudice* from the publisher, 'in the evening we set fairly at it and read half the first vol.'. There must have been many other occasions when Jane shared her work in this room.

Revd Austen's bookcase

The bureau-bookcase belonged to the Reverend George Austen and was bought by the Jane Austen Society in 1950 from Sotheby's. The National Art Collections Fund contributed to the cost. It was the Society's first major purchase.

1810 Clementi square piano

In a corner of the drawing room is a piano – not the actual one on which Jane practised every morning, but an instrument of the same period. This piano can be played by visitors to the Museum and is also used for concerts and recitals.

'Yes, yes we will have a piano forte,
as good a one as can be got for 30 guineas.'

Jane's niece, Caroline Austen, remembered that 'Aunt Jane began her day with music... she chose her practicing time before breakfast when she could have the room to herself.'

The Museum holds a number of the manuscript music books, which Jane copied out for herself 'so neatly and correctly, that it was as easy to read as print.'

Duke of Yorks March

A selection of the 'Knight' china in the Dining Parlour

The Dining Parlour

Although Cassandra took on most of the management of the Austen ladies' household, Jane prepared breakfast and was in charge of tea and coffee, which were kept locked away in the cupboard by the fireplace. While the family's main meals would have been cooked in the kitchen, the breakfast would have been prepared over the small range-like grate in the dining parlour.

Also in the dining parlour is part of the dinner service that belonged to Jane's brother, Edward. Jane accompanied Edward and her niece, Fanny, when they went to purchase the china at the Wedgwood showrooms in London, as she describes it in a letter to Cassandra.

> ***'We then went to Wedgwoods where my Br & Fanny chose a Dinner Set. - I believe the pattern is a small Lozenge in purple, between Lines of narrow Gold; & it is to have the Crest.'***
>
> **Letter to Cassandra, 16 September 1813**

Jane spent her mornings in this room writing and revising and although her family knew of her literary work it was not widely broadcast at the time. In her lifetime, Jane earned just £808 from her writing.

Writing Table

This 12-sided piece of walnut on a single tripod is the table where Jane established herself as a writer at Chawton. In her younger days at Steventon, Jane wrote upstairs however, at Chawton, she wrote near the little-used front door, and here she wrote 'upon small sheets of paper which could easily be put away, or covered with a piece of blotting paper'. A creaking swing door gave her warning when anyone was coming, and it is said that she refused to have the creak fixed.

Jane wrote letters as well as revising her earlier manuscripts and from this table it is believed came *Mansfield Park*, *Emma* and *Persuasion*.

After Jane's death Mrs Austen gave the table to a manservant but eventually it was returned to its old home once the house had become a Museum.

Jane also owned a 'writing slope' which was passed down through the family and is now in the British Library.

Topaz Crosses

In 1801 the HMS *Endymion* made port at Portsmouth and Jane's brother Lieutenant Charles Austen arrived bearing gifts for his two sisters – two topaz crosses and gold chains purchased in Gibraltar from his share of prize money from the capture of a French vessel, the *Scipio*, in the Mediterranean. In a similar incident in *Mansfield Park* Fanny Price receives an amber cross from her sailor brother, William.

'The Endymion *came into Portsmouth on Sunday, & I have sent Charles a short letter by this day's post…He has received 30£ for his share of the privateer & expects 10£ more – but of what avail is it to take prizes if he lays out the produce in presents to his Sisters. He has been buying Gold chains & Topaze Crosses for us; – he must be well scolded…I shall write again by this post to thank and reproach him. We shall be unbearably fine.'*

Letter to Cassandra, 27 May 1801

The Vestibule

The Vestibule area of the house is much altered from the days when the Austens lived at Chawton, as a result of the house being divided up into a number of dwellings after Cassandra's death.

The front door once led into this area and the window is a later addition. The fireplace, too large for such a small area, has been altered at some point in the house's history.

The portrait above the fireplace is of Jane's brother, Edward, as a teenaged boy, possibly painted when he first went to live with the Knight cousins, whose heir he became. A larger portrait of Edward as a young man, a copy of which can be seen here, is now on display at Chawton House. Edward changed his name to Knight in 1812 after inheriting the Knight estates.

'We have reason to suppose the change of name has taken place, as we have to forward a Letter to Edward Knight Esqre …I must learn to make a better K.'

Letter to Martha Lloyd, 29 November 1812

The display case in this area is used for changing displays including manuscript letters by Jane Austen, her music books and other rarely seen items. In the drawers below are the topaz crosses given to Jane and Cassandra by their brother Charles, and other family memorabilia.

The Reading Room

We do not know the exact use in the Austens' day of the room we now call the Reading Room although it was once referred to as 'offices'. Until recently it was our bookshop, but it is now used to house our collection of reference books. Revd Austen had a large library at Steventon, however many of his books were sold before the move to Bath and it is unlikely that the Reading Room would have been used for this purpose.

Today the Reading Room houses a large collection of reference books and other material for research and enjoyment of visitors. Here too you will find our ever-growing collection of foreign language editions of Jane's work.

Jane and Cassandra's Bedroom

The upstairs rooms have changed in their configuration and would have been very different before the house was split up.

We do not know for certain the arrangements of the 'six bedchambers' at Chawton and who slept where, however Jane and Cassandra had shared a bedroom at Steventon and it is believed did so again once they moved to Chawton. In a letter to Martha Lloyd, when she is away from Chawton, Jane tells her that during a visit from Edward and his family, Edward had been given the 'ample space of yours' suggesting that Martha occupied one of the larger rooms.

The tent bed displayed in the Museum was recreated from the details known about the beds Revd Austen had made for his daughters in 1794 by Ring Brothers of Basingstoke while the family lived at Steventon Rectory. Although the room seems small to have held two such beds, in Jane's time bedchambers were only used for sleeping.

The closet in the corner of the room contains a chamber pot and a washbowl, which sits in the hole cut into the shelf. The upper shelf is cut away for headroom. There were no bathrooms in houses in Jane's day and warm water would have been brought up from the kitchen by a maidservant.

Jane's niece Caroline recalled seeing her Aunt Jane for the last time sitting by the fireplace in her bedroom when she was too ill to go downstairs. 'She was in her dressing gown and was sitting quite like an invalid in an armchair.'

A few days before Jane moved to Winchester for medical treatment she wrote 'I have kept my bed since 13. April with only removals to a Sopha [sic].'

Below: Lace collar worked by Jane and a sampler worked by Cassandra

The Austen Family Room

Mrs Austen is believed to have occupied this front bedroom, which is today used to display items of memorabilia belonging to the Austen family.

Small items of jewellery are displayed including some which contain locks of hair from deceased family members. Hair jewellery could remind loved ones of each other when they were apart or serve as a memento of a friend or family member who had died. It was common to save locks of hair and weave them into bracelets, brooches and rings. On display are brooches containing Jane's hair and that of her father.

Above the fireplace is the portrait of John Austen, great-grandfather of Jane. This is believed to be the earliest portrait of a member of the Austen line.

Martha Lloyd's Recipe Book

Martha Lloyd's household book is a book full of handwritten recipes, household advice, medicinal remedies and formulas.

Martha Lloyd came to live with Mrs Austen, Cassandra and Jane at Southampton after the death of her own mother and later moved with them to Chawton.

The household book was probably started by Martha in her younger years and she continued to add to it during her time in Southampton and at Chawton. The book contains recipes from many different members of the Austen family and their circle of friends, though there are none in the handwriting we recognise as Jane's.

Martha continued to collect recipes after her marriage to Francis Austen and their move to Portsdown Lodge.

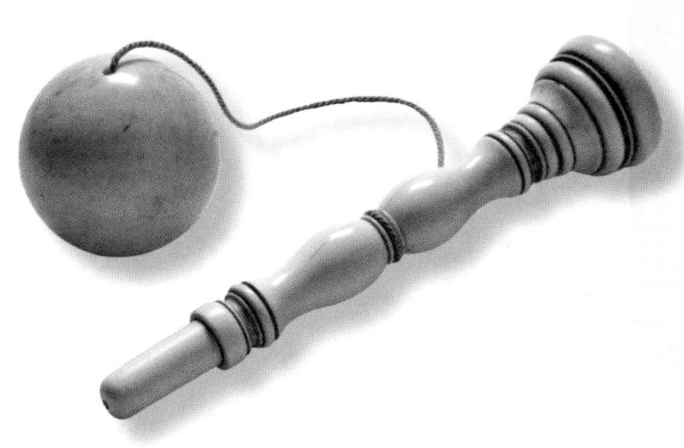

Cup-and-Ball

Cup-and-ball (or ball-in-a-cup) is a traditional children's toy consisting of a wooden cup with a handle, and a ball attached to the cup by a string. This ivory cup-and-ball was believed to have belonged to Jane, who was very skilful at the game.

> *'Her performances with the cup-and-ball were marvellous. She has been known to catch the ball on the point above a hundred times in succession.'*
>
> **James Edward Austen-Leigh**

The Dressing Room

This small room may have been used as a dressing room or a bedroom for visiting nieces and nephews.

In this room is an account of the many houses and places that Jane lived in or visited including Steventon, Bath, Southampton, Godmersham, Chawton and Winchester.

The display cases show Austen-related items of dress including satin slippers, fans, a shawl given to Jane by Edward's mother-in-law, and intricately worked handkerchiefs. One handkerchief was made for Edward by his sisters and one, with Cassandra's initials, was worked by Jane. There is also a needle case made by Jane for her niece, Louisa, with the handmade wrapper bearing the words 'With Aunt Jane's love'.

Another display cabinet holds items found under the floorboards of the house, including a small wooden plane dating from 1690, which may have been lost when the house was built or extended, a penknife used for making quill pen nibs, items of cutlery and a small toy cannon.

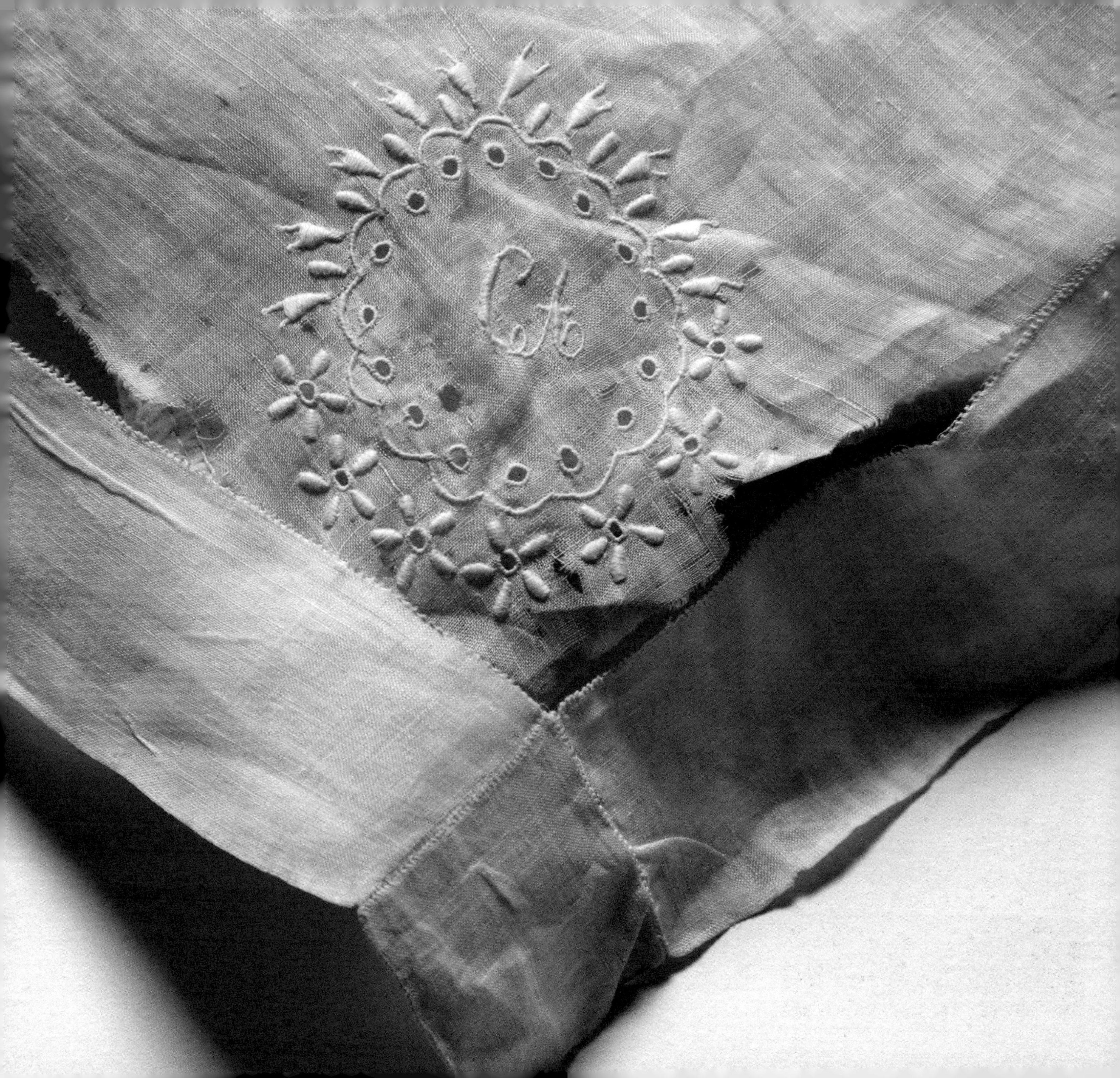

Burmese Bell

The Burmese Bell was presented to Jane's brother Charles;

> *'Presented by Captors of the storming of Rangoon 14th April 1852 to Rear Admiral Austen C.B. Commander in Chief of the Naval Force employed as that occasion and left by him at Admiralty House Trincomalee, as an heir-loom.'*

The bell eventually came to the Museum in 1985 after having been held in several offices of the Royal Navy. The Bell is so heavy that it took five naval ratings to carry it up the stairs to the Admirals' room.

The Admirals' Room

This room contains memorabilia of Jane's two sailor brothers, Francis and Charles. Both brothers joined the Royal Navy at the age of 12. Francis became Admiral of the Fleet and was knighted by King William IV after a long distinguished career. Francis lived to be ninety-one.

The cabin bed seen here belonged to Francis and was taken by him on all his voyages.

Charles Austen, Jane's 'own particular little brother', became a Rear Admiral and served in conflicts in North American waters, South America and the Far East. Charles died at the age of seventy-three, so both brothers had many years of activity and service.

The cupboard contains some of the Austen family silver, in particular a snuff box and salver presented to Charles Austen by his brother officers. There are also examples of wood carvings by Francis.

Francis Austen

Ceremonial sword presented to Charles Austen

Charles Austen was serving on the HMS *Aurora* in 1827 when he was presented with a naval sword bearing the inscription: 'Presented to Charles John Austen R.N. commanding HMS *Aurora* at the city of Caracas, 1st March 1827 by General Simon Bolivar the liberator of his country as a mark of esteem'. It is uncertain what personal service Charles rendered but the sword was probably presented to him, the senior naval officer at Caracas, as a token of gratitude for Britain's continuing support for Bolivar's political ambitions.

The Bedroom Tableau

This small room was probably once a dressing room serving the larger bedroom next door. The travelling trunk was once owned by Edward Knight.

The bed is a reproduction tent bed used here to display the patchwork coverlet worked by Jane, Cassandra and Mrs Austen.

The red felt jacket belonged to Mrs Austen and was cut down and reworked to make a riding jacket for Francis when he was seven.

Also displayed is a pair of pattens. Pattens were worn outdoors over normal shoes and were held in place by leather or cloth bands. Pattens were to raise the foot above the mud in wet weather at a time when paving was rare.

The Corridor and Alcove

The window in the alcove looks out over the fork in the road by the thatched cottage. In Jane's day all traffic for Winchester or Alton would have passed through Chawton as there was no bypass. There was a large village pond by the thatched cottage

By the window seat is a framed copy and transcript of the letter that Cassandra wrote to her niece, Fanny Knight, telling her of her Aunt Jane's death.

> *'I have lost a treasure, such a Sister, such a friend as never can have been surpassed – she was the sun of my life, the gilder of every pleasure, the soother of every sorrow, I had not a thought concealed from her, & it is as if I had lost a part of myself.'*

Letter from Cassandra to Fanny Knight, 18 July 1818

The Quilt

The Quilt was made by Mrs Austen, Jane and Cassandra.

In a letter to Cassandra on 31 May 1811 Jane writes 'have you remembered to collect peices (sic) for the Patchwork? – we are now at a standstill.'

The quilt has just two layers – the patchwork top and a backing but no wadding, so is a coverlet rather than a quilt.

The patchwork uses 64 different fabrics and was created using two sizes of lozenge diamond, and a rhomboid shape of black-and-white spotted fabric for the lattice effect which divides the diamonds.

There is a central diamond-shaped floral motif, which features a basket of flowers, and surrounding this are sequences of four diamond-shaped patches. Around the edges is a border of smaller diamond patches displaying landscapes and flowers.

The quilt was one of the earliest items in the Museum collection.

The Kitchen, Bakehouse and the Well

In Jane's time the Kitchen was attached to the house, though entered through a separate door to the main rooms. The Bakehouse, as today, was separate from the main building and would have been a very important part of the domestic domain of the cottage. The activities that took place in the Bakehouse would have included baking, washing clothes and salting pigs.

Just outside the Bakehouse is a well. It is believed that in Jane's time a second well was also available, though the position of this is no longer known.

The well was needed to provide the water for the household and particularly for the laundry. The copper was used for washing clothes and linen. A fire would be lit underneath and the clothes boiled in the upper compartment, now covered with a wooden lid. Jane even sent a

Above: The well is still being used today to measure the water table in East Hampshire

parcel of clothes home from London where she was staying with her brother Henry:

> ***'I want to get rid of some of my Things, & therefore shall send down a parcel by Collier on Saturday... It will be mostly dirty Cloathes.'***
>
> **Letter to Cassandra, 17 October 1815**

The baking for the Austen household took place here too. The proximity of the well and the copper made the Bakehouse the perfectly practical place for boiling water for scalding the skins of slaughtered pigs.

The cellar below the Bakehouse would have been used to store salted foods prior to their use in the kitchen.

The Donkey Carriage

Jane was a 'desperate walker' but her mother's Donkey Carriage would have been used for shopping trips and other slightly longer journeys. Unlike a coach the carriage offered no protection against bad weather

> ***'Mary Jane and I have been wet through once already today, we set off in the Donkey Carriage for Farringdon ... but were obliged to turn back before we got there, but not soon enough to avoid a Pelter all the way home.'***
>
> **Letter to James Edward, 9 July 1816**

At the end of her life Jane made more frequent use of the Donkey Carriage, though in order to be more independent and less 'troublesome' by not always using the carriage Jane took to riding one of their donkeys.

> ***'I have a scheme however for accomplishing more, as the weather grows more springlike. I mean to take up riding the donkey... I shall be able to go about with Cassandra in her walks to Alton & Wyards.'***
>
> **Letter to Fanny Knight, 13 March 1817**

The Garden

The original form of the garden at Jane Austen's House is not known. The plot of land with the house would have been larger, covering several acres in the Austen's time however, over the years parts of the land have been sold off and the original outline has been obscured.

James Edward Austen-Leigh in his memoir of his aunt recalled the garden:

> ***'A high wooden fence and hornbeam hedge shut out the Winchester road... Trees were planted each side to form a shrubbery walk, carried round the enclosure, which gave sufficient space for ladies' exercise.'***

He also recalled 'a pleasant irregular mixture of hedgerow, and gravel walk, and orchard, and long grass for mowing.'

The years of living at Steventon would have prepared Jane and Cassandra for a level of what today would be called self-sufficiency. Much of what they ate came from their garden and orchard and they also kept chickens and turkeys as well as harvesting honey from bees.

Jane took pleasure in their garden and when Cassandra was away from Chawton Jane included details of what was happening in the garden in her letters.

> ***'... the whole of the shrubbery border will soon be very gay with Pinks & Sweet Williams, in addition to the Colombines already in bloom. The Syringas too are coming out.'***
>
> **Letter to Cassandra, 29 May 1811**

The garden was to an extent neglected in the years after the house was broken up into workers cottages. In a letter to *The Times* in 1926 one of the tenants of the cottages, Edith Hall wrote: 'When we came here we found a large piece of ground which had nothing but rubbish and weeds on it, and we spent the first year cleaning it all out. Now it has been cultivated into beds of flowers etc., which makes it a picture of beauty in the summer months'. She also mentions that the area of garden allocated to the St Nicholas Club was in a very bad state of neglect.

In the early years as a museum the garden was laid out according to a design by Selwyn Duruz. Design for a garden for Jane Austen's

House was published in a pamphlet at the time of the opening of the Museum in 1949. Duruz questioned the sort of garden Jane Austen would have known and concluded:

> ***'Probably it will have resembled the type of happy mixture of bettered cottage garden one associates with old rectories and vicarages.'***

By 1950 the Jane Austen Society was able to report that:

> ***'All summer, and well into the autumn, [the garden] was gay with flowers that Jane Austen would have known, including those mentioned in her letters; syringa, laburnum, peony and mignonette.'***

The garden has been enhanced in recent years to include many period varieties of plants. The gardener aims to choose plants and shrubs that would only have been available to the Austens when they were living here; for example, there is a bed of plants used in the dying process near to the house. Tickseed produces a yellow, green or rust colour. Madder, which produces a red, and even onion skins which produce yellow or rust, were used for dying.

The garden also contains many edible and medicinal herbs however the kitchen garden was lost when the Learning Centre was built in 2009. The gardener continues to mix vegetables into the flower borders in a way that surprises and delights visitors, though this may be in keeping with the garden in the time of the Austen women.

Today the garden supplies a regular bounty of fresh flowers, which are arranged and placed around the Museum enhancing the feeling of a real home.

THE GARDEN PATH

When the cottage first became a museum the flag stones that had once been the floor of the kitchen were obtained to create a path along the side of the house to prevent gravel and grit being trodden into the drawing room. The stones had for some years been used in another estate cottage on the other side of the street. In 2009 this path was taken up again and the flagstones relaid in the Historic Kitchen. A new path was laid in the garden.

Is this Jane Austen?
A recently discovered portrait

The Legacy of Jane Austen

Jane Austen's writing was of pivotal importance for the modern novel. Without Jane we would not be reading novels in the way that we do today. In a time when it was considered that sermons, travel books and books on manners and behaviour were the proper things to read the Austen family were a family of novel readers and proud of it.

Jane Austen's first biographer was her brother Henry, who contributed a Biographical Note to the posthumously published set of *Persuasion* and *Northanger Abbey* in 1818. These few paragraphs identified Jane for the first time as the author of her previously published works, all of which had been issued anonymously, stating the author to be 'A Lady', or later citing her as the author of one of her previous titles. After the initial sales all of Jane's books went out of print and remained so until late 1832. Since then the novels of Jane Austen have been continuously in print.

In 1869 Jane's nephew, James Edward Austen-Leigh, published a biography of his 'dear aunt Jane'. Although now considered to be a romanticised view of Jane, Austen-Leigh's biography generated public interest, and the novels were swiftly reissued. Routledge published the first popular editions in 1883; followed by illustrated and collected versions.

Today numerous adaptations, prequels, sequels, comic books, zombie mash-ups and more have been based on the novels of Jane Austen. This is nothing new; family members began the trend in the middle of the nineteenth century writing conclusions to the incomplete novels.

The first film adaptation was the 1940 MGM production of *Pride and Prejudice* starring Laurence Olivier and Greer Garson. The BBC and ITV have adapted the novels on a number of occasions, starting with one produced in the 1970s. The 1995 BBC production of *Pride and Prejudice*, which starred Jennifer Ehle and Colin Firth, is still talked about and popular today.

Bibliography

A Chronology of Jane Austen and her Family – Deirdre Le Faye (Cambridge 2006)

Jane Austen: A Family Record – William Austen-Leigh & Deirdre Le Faye (London 1989)

Jane Austen's Letters – ed. Deirdre Le Faye (Oxford 1995)

The History of Jane Austen's House: Some Highlights – Lareme Jones (Chawton 2006)

In the Garden with Jane Austen – Kim Wilson & Celia Simpson (London 2009)

Thanks and Acknowledgements

Chesil Theatre, Winchester. www.chesiltheatre.org.uk

Jane Hurst for the use of her extensive research on the history of the house which is today Jane Austen's House Museum.

Dr Paula Byrne for permission to reproduce the portrait on page 46.

Staff and stewards at Jane Austen's House Museum for their help in bringing this book to fruition.

Text by Madelaine Smith
Published by Jigsaw Design & Publishing Ltd, Norwich

Photography by Peter Smith of Newbery Smith Photography Ltd.
except John Crook (p5 bottom right)
Archive material provided by Jane Austen's House Museum
www.jigsaw-publishing.co.uk
Printed in Great Britain by Swallowtail Print.
11047-1/12 ISBN 978-1-907750-36-6

The opening lines of *Pride and Prejudice* are some of the most frequently quoted (and misquoted) words in the English language and are used in numerous contexts that have nothing to do with the original books. 'Mr Darcy' has become shorthand for all that is desirable in a husband.

From a small table in a modest dining room in a cottage in a Hampshire village, the words of Jane Austen have been heard the world over.